ISSUES IN OUR WORLD

TERRORISM

Helen Donohoe

Aladdin / Watts
London • Sydney

ABOUT THIS BOOK

TERRORISM is an issue that can put us all in danger. This book will help you to understand why terrorism happens. Learn about the effects of terrorism around the world. Look at how governments are trying to create a safer world for us all.

© Aladdin Books Ltd 2007
Produced by Aladdin Books Ltd
2/3 Fitzroy Mews, London W1T 6DF

ISBN 978–07496–7487–8

First published in 2007 by

Franklin Watts	Franklin Watts Australia
338 Euston Road	Level 17/207 Kent Street
London NW1 3BH	Sydney NSW 2000

Franklin Watts is a division of Hachette Children's Books.

Designers: Flick, Book Design and Graphics
Pete Bennett – PBD
Editor: Katie Dicker
Editorial consultant: Professor Stuart Croft, Department of Political Science and International Studies, University of Birmingham, UK.

The author, Helen Donohoe, has an MA in politics and writes for a wide audience, including senior politicians and journalists.

Printed in Malaysia   All rights reserved

A CIP catalogue record for this book is available from the British Library.
Dewey Classification: 303.6'25

CONTENTS

INTRODUCTION

Stories of terrorist attacks are always in the news. Today, we are asking more than ever before, why terrorism occurs, and how it can be prevented.

Terrorism alters many lives. The passion and anger felt by the communities affected never goes away. This is why terrorism will always be a feature of the news.

The Omagh bomb affected both Catholics and Protestants.

Lockerbie 1988

In December 1988, a plane flying from London to New York exploded over the Scottish town of Lockerbie. It killed 270 people. In 2001, Abdel Baset Al Megrahi, a Libyan intelligence agent, was found guilty of the bombing.

Omagh 1998

In August 1998, a bomb exploded in a shopping street in Omagh, Northern Ireland. It killed 29 people and injured at least 220. This attack was linked to a group called the 'Real IRA'.

September 11th

The terrorist attacks in the US on 11 September 2001 were on a scale that has never been seen before. Over 3,000 people died. But terrorism is not new.

Throughout history, people have used terror to achieve their goals. Terrorist attacks are often caused by differences in religious beliefs or political ideals. People everywhere need to learn how to deal with the threat of violence.

A worker searches the remains of the World Trade Center in New York in 2001.

Guy Fawkes

In 1604, a group of Englishmen began to plot against James I. They didn't like the King because he was punishing Catholics. The men tried to blow up the House of Lords to kill James I.

However, the King's men found out about the plan. On 4 November 1605, a man named Guy Fawkes was found with lots of gunpowder. In 1606, Guy Fawkes and the other plotters were killed because they were traitors.

TERRORISM IN HISTORY

Terrorism has the same causes whether we talk about the Guy Fawkes plot of 1605 or the terrorist threats of today.

Terrorism happens because different people, with opposite views, live side by side. Terrorists are beginning to use different methods to achieve their goals. To deal with the threat of terrorism, countries are using stricter rules to try to keep people safe.

WHAT TERRORISM IS

Terrorism is the use of violence or threats to achieve something. A terrorist might try to influence a government or change the behaviour of a group of people. An extreme act involving widespread destruction, like that of 11 September 2001, is a clear example of terrorism at its worst.

The twin towers of the World Trade Center.

In 2001, two hijacked planes crashed into the World Trade Center.

THE WORD TERRORISM

The term 'terrorism' was first used in 1795, to describe the French government's *Reign of Terror*. This was when many presumed enemies of the government were killed. Gradually the word 'terrorism' was used to describe all violent activity. In the late 19th century, the word 'terrorist' was used to describe revolutionary movements in Ireland and Russia.

Terrorism is defined in some laws. In the UK, terrorism is 'the use of action to influence a government or intimidate the public for political, religious or ideological reasons'. The UK Terrorism Act 2006 adds new offences and changes others.

On 11 September 2001, another hijacked plane crashed into the Pentagon in Washington DC, killing nearly 200.

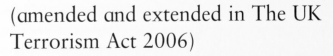

11 September 2001

On 11 September 2001, four US flights were hijacked. Two planes were diverted to New York. They crashed into the World Trade Center towers, which collapsed. The third plane crashed into the Pentagon in Washington DC. The fourth crashed in woodland in Pennsylvania. Everyone onboard died.

Different opinions

It is often said that one person's terrorist is another person's freedom fighter. Somebody who uses violence to influence a government may be fighting to help a group of people. It can also be difficult to separate the work of political activists and terrorists. In Northern Ireland, for example, some political parties share similar views to terrorist groups (see page 34).

Terrorism is mostly started by religious, social or political movements. This is the difference between terrorism and other types of violence, such as murder or football hooliganism.

Terrorism Act 2000

(amended and extended in The UK Terrorism Act 2006)

Establishing laws against terrorism is very difficult. The latest UK anti-terrorism law avoids this problem by listing 21 terrorist organisations by name. Membership of these groups is illegal in the UK. The list includes six Islamic groups and four anti-Israel groups. One of these is the military part of Hezbollah. Hezbollah is also a legal political party in the Middle Eastern country of Lebanon.

7

Politics in action

Acts of terrorism often involve death and devastation. Many people would say this is also a common theme of 'war'. Other people think that the bombing of Lebanon by Israel in 2006 was not far from an act of terrorism. Another example is the use of radioactive weapons by British and American forces in the invasion of Iraq. These weapons cause cancer. However, it is still very difficult to define terrorism today.

Government support

Terrorism is often aimed at the actions of governments. However, some governments have been blamed for supporting terrorist activities.

In 2003, the US accused a number of countries in the Middle East of supporting terrorism with money and weapons. However, the US (and Britain) also have a history of supporting terrorism.

In 1979, when Russia invaded Afghanistan, the US supported the 'Mujahideen'. This was a group of fighters who were against the communist invasion of the area.

When the Soviet army left in 1989, the US withdrew their support for the Mujahideen. Some members of this group have since formed the al-Qaeda network (see page 16). They have turned against their former American supporters.

However, like individuals, governments can also have a change of heart. In December 2003, the Libyan leader, Colonel Gaddafi, said that his country would not support terrorists anymore.

8

THE CAUSES OF TERRORISM

Terrorism is often caused by very strong feelings of injustice. Some people think that there are no alternative ways to solve a problem. Terrorism can be caused by arguments over land or territory. It can also be caused by different cultural or religious beliefs or feelings of political or economic inequality.

Religion was the cause of terrorist attacks in the former Yugoslavia.

Israelis and Palestinians are fighting about religion and land.

RELIGIOUS TERRORISM

There has been a conflict between Arab Muslims and Jews throughout history. In the time of the Bible, Jewish people lived on the land that is now known as Israel. But in 800 AD, this area came under Arab rule. Many Jews were forced to leave. The Jewish people still think this area is their 'homeland'. In the early 1900s, thousands started to move back.

The creation of Israel

The argument got worse in 1948, when Israel and Palestine were created. In the Second World War, millions of Jews were killed by the German Nazi regime. Israel was created as a country where surviving Jews could live. The United Nations (UN) decided to split Palestine into two states: Palestine (Arab) and Israel (Jewish). Over 700,000 Palestinians were forced to leave their homes. This caused tensions between Israelis and Palestinians. The main areas of land that are currently being disputed are known as the West Bank and the Gaza Strip.

Green – Mainly Palestinians
Blue – Mainly Israelis
Striped – Disputed land

10

Suicide bombers target buses in Israel.

Conflict in Israel

• An international peace process began in 1993 to try to resolve the conflict between Palestinians and Israelis.
• In 1995, Israeli Prime Minister Yitzhak Rabin was killed by a Jewish religious extremist.
• In 1996, the disputes continued with a number of suicide bombings in Israel. These were carried out by Islamic groups such as Hamas.
• The terrorist attacks continue to this day.

DISPUTES OVER LAND

Most Chechen people come from a Muslim population. For centuries, they lived in the mountains in Russia. However, during the Second World War, Stalin accused the Chechens of co-operating with the Nazis. He forced the Chechen population to move to Kazakhstan. They moved back to Russia after Stalin died.

An ongoing conflict

In 1991, Chechnya declared that it was independent from Russia. Three years later, Boris Yeltsin (the president of Russia at the time) sent Russian troops to take back control in Chechnya. A war

Freedom fighters

In 2002, Chechen terrorists attacked a theatre in Moscow. They took 800 people hostage. Russian troops stormed the theatre. However, the gas they used to stop the terrorists killed more than 120 hostages as well as some of the terrorists. The Chechen rebels acted because they wanted political independence.

began which killed about 80,000 people. In 1996, Chechnya became partly independent from Russia. Now Chechens want full independence. This ongoing conflict has led to an uprising of Chechen rebel terrorists.

11

Chechen rebels (left) have been linked to many terrorist attacks in Russia.

Chechnya and al-Qaeda

Since 2000, many Chechens have moved away. Lots of people have been killed in the fighting and poverty is widespread.

It is now thought that Chechen rebels are supported by al-Qaeda. Many Muslims have gone to Chechnya to join the fight. They have been to training camps linked with al-Qaeda. Some Chechens also fought with al-Qaeda and Taliban forces against the US-led invasion of Afghanistan in 2001.

Chechnya facts

• Chechnya has around one million citizens.
• The population of Chechnya is mainly Muslim.
• Chechnya wants independence from Russia, but Russia wants to keep it.

A member of the Northern Alliance looks for al-Qaeda suspects during the US-led invasion of Afghanistan in 2001.

POLITICAL TERRORISM

Political terrorism is often carried out by extreme groups who do not like a particular political system.

In April 1995, a bomb in Oklahoma, USA, killed 168 people.

Oklahoma, USA

Before 11 September 2001, the Oklahoma bomb in April 1995 was the biggest single act of terrorism in the US. It killed 168 people. Timothy McVeigh carried out the attack. He was executed in 2001.

McVeigh was born in 1968 in New York State. He began collecting guns at school. He became fascinated by political and racist literature. McVeigh thought that Americans were under threat of attack, from communists or the central government. He was particularly distressed by the Ruby Ridge catastrophe in 1992. This was when a siege by police killed the wife of racist Randy Weaver and their 14-year-old son (see page 14).

Waco, Texas

In 1993, David Koresh, the leader of a religious cult, died in a fire with more than 80 of his followers. The US government had seized the cult's compound in Waco, Texas. The government thought that Koresh was abusing the several children he fathered with his followers.

McVeigh was upset by the Waco siege. No one knows what caused McVeigh to plant the Oklahoma bomb. But the bombing changed the way that Americans looked at terrorism. At first, Middle Eastern organisations were blamed. However, Americans soon realised the terrorist threat was within their own country.

14

It took six weeks for rescuers to find the victims of Oklahoma.

The Oklahoma bomb – key dates

• 1968 – Timothy McVeigh born, New York.
• 1992 – Police forces storm the home of a racist man called Randy Weaver at Ruby Ridge, Idaho. Weaver's wife Vicki and their son, Sammy, are killed.
• 1993 – McVeigh visits Waco, Texas, where a 51-day police siege ends with 82 people killed.
• 1995 – At 09:02 am on 19 April, a van packed with home-made explosives, blows up in Oklahoma City. McVeigh is caught and charged with the bombing.
• 2001 – McVeigh is executed by lethal injection.

MORAL BELIEFS

Terrorism can also be caused by a belief that there are rights and wrongs in society. Some terrorists believe that people in power are not taking enough action to punish 'wrongdoers'.

Anti-abortion

One of these issues is abortion. The US has a long history of anti-abortion activity. At first this was just non-violent protests. But in the late 1980s, America began to experience more violent attacks. The targets were abortion clinics and the staff working in them.

A wanted man

Eric Robert Rudolph is one of the most famous anti-abortion terrorists in the US. In 1998, he was suspected of bombing the Centennial Olympic Park at the 1996 Atlanta Olympics. The attack killed one and injured 111 others. Rudolph was also charged with bombing a health clinic in Birmingham, Alabama, USA. In 2005, Rudolph was given five life sentences.

Animal protection

Animal rights is another cause of terrorism. Groups have vandalised laboratories, stolen animals, used bombs or threatened employees. This activity disrupts work and costs employers a lot of money.

Abortion was legalised in the US in the 1970s. However, anti-abortion groups campaign against it.

15

AL-QAEDA

Al-Qaeda is the world's first international terrorist network. It offers support for a number of radical Islamic terrorist groups. These groups don't like the ownership of land in Muslim countries. They are also against the role of the US and its western allies in the Middle East.

The al-Qaeda network was started by a Saudi Arabian called Osama bin Laden. Al-Qaeda has organised training camps for thousands of terrorists. The network actively supported the Taliban against the US in Afghanistan in 2001. Al-Qaeda is now thought to be working against the US control and restructuring of Iraq.

The events of 11 September 2001 saw al-Qaeda take their activities to the US. Many terrorist groups are now working with al-Qaeda. They are helping to spread its activities throughout the world.

September 2001 – Nineteen suicide attackers hijack and crash four US aeroplanes. The attacks, which claimed more than 3,000 lives, were linked to al-Qaeda.

October 2002 – Two car bombs in Bali kill more than 200 and injure more than 300. An Islamic group linked to al-Qaeda was blamed.

July 2005 – Suicide bombers kill 53 people in four attacks in London. One was on a bus and three were on underground trains.

August 2006 – A massive security alert at UK airports prevents suspected attacks on flights to the US.

Osama bin Laden is the main suspect of the September 2001 attacks. He has not been found

THE TERRORISTS' TOOLS

Terrorists achieve their aims in a number of ways. Terrorist attacks vary from targeting individuals to harming large groups of people. Attacks on public transport are very effective. These attacks disrupt daily life. They can cost a government millions. The attacks also get a lot of publicity.

The wreckage of the Lockerbie bomb. The bomb exploded on an aeroplane over Scotland in 1988.

Hijacking

In the 1970s, over 30% of terrorist attacks were hijacked aircraft. In September 2001, the hijacking of four aircraft in the US showed that hijacking is still useful to terrorists.

Aeroplanes are also a popular target for bombers. Explosives (activated by timing devices) can kill all those onboard. Suicide bombers are also a serious threat.

In December 2001, a US flight made an emergency landing in Boston. A passenger had tried to set off explosives hidden in his shoes. Richard Reid (the 'shoe bomber') had links with al-Qaeda. He was sentenced to life in prison in 2003.

Bombs

Bombs are very popular with terrorists. They are easy to use and transport. They also have serious effects. Plastic explosives are small, light and do not smell. Bombs can also be fitted with timing devices.

In 1984, the Irish Republican Army (IRA) targeted the Grand Hotel in Brighton, UK. The Conservative government were there for their annual party conference. The terrorists planted a bomb weeks before the event to avoid any security checks.

Car bombs

Car bombs have been used to kill politicians (see page 19). They can also do a lot of damage. In 2002, a car bomb exploded in a tourist area in Bali, Indonesia. It killed over 200 people. An Islamic group known to have links with al-Qaeda was blamed. In 2006, over 100 Sri Lankan sailors died and over 100 were injured in a truck bomb attack near the capital Colombo.

Car bombs cause a lot of damage.

Suicide bombers

Some suicide bombers carry explosives on their body. Others drive a vehicle packed with explosives. They kill themselves and people around them. Suicide bombers make people very scared. Accurate, large-scale attacks can also be carried out very easily.

Suicide bombings are particularly common in the Middle East. This is because many suicide bombers are influenced by religious beliefs. According to Islamic tradition, people who give their life for an Islamic cause will have their sins forgiven. They believe this will grant them a place in paradise.

Assassinations

Some terrorist attacks have specific targets. In 1979, the UK Shadow Northern Ireland Secretary, Airey Neave, was killed by a car bomb. Splinter groups of the IRA (see page 46) attacked Neave because of his anti-IRA security policies. Neave was killed just before the Conservatives came to power, when he would have joined the British Cabinet.

Hostages

Terrorists have also used sieges to try to influence governments. In 1979, a group of radical Iranian students stormed the American Embassy in Tehran. They took the staff hostage for over a year.

The students were angered by US support for their exiled leader, the Shah. They were supported by the Iranian government.

Beirut, Lebanon

In 1986, Brian Keenan and ten other westerners were captured by terrorists in Beirut. Some hostages were held for over five years.

19

Staff at the American Embassy in Tehran were taken hostage in 1979.

Information

Terrorist groups, such as al-Qaeda, share information with other terrorist groups. Sometimes, this support is planned. At other times, it is accidental. Modern technology, such as the internet, means that ideas can be shared very easily.

Al-Qaeda have used training camps in Afghanistan.

Newspaper reports spread the work of terrorists around the world.

News coverage

News reports and images of terrorist attacks reach people around the world very quickly. When the knowledge spreads, so does fear. Many people now live in fear of a terrorist threat. However, the risk to themselves is actually very small.

Baader-Meinhof

The Baader-Meinhof gang was a terrorist group of young middle-class German people. They wanted to change the political system of their country. They were officially known as the Red Army Faction in Germany in the 1970s. They carried out a series of kidnappings, robberies and bombings.

The Baader-Meinhof were initially trained in the Middle East. At the time, groups like the PLO (see page 46) were trying to spread their cause. The Baader-Meinhof gang broke up in the early 1990s.

20

TYPES OF TERRORISTS

It is difficult to know what a typical terrorist looks like. Terrorists act for many different reasons. They may be driven by poverty or a lack of opportunities. They may have different political or religious beliefs.

Osama bin Laden, leader of the al-Qaeda network.

Different backgrounds

Terrorists have also come from wealthy and well educated backgrounds. For example, Osama bin Laden, the leader of the al-Qaeda network, was born into great wealth. It is believed that he inherited as much as US$300 million when his father died in the 1960s. Osama bin Laden is the world's most wanted terrorist.

Middle-class terrorists

Andreas Baader was the son of a historian. He formed the Red Army Faction with Ulrike Meinhof. He was captured in 1972. Baader committed suicide in 1977.

21

Ulrike Meinhof was the daughter of an art historian. She graduated in philosophy and sociology. She was a writer for political magazines. Meinhof was captured by police in 1972. She committed suicide in 1976.

Terrorist groups in Israel recruit young people who show an interest in Islam.

A lawyer's son

Mohammed Atta was one of the terrorists who flew a plane into the World Trade Center in September 2001. He was from a wealthy background. He was the son of a successful lawyer in a middle-class area in Cairo, Egypt.

A young girl

In 2002, Shinaz Amuri set off a bomb in Jerusalem. She killed herself, an old man and injured more than 100 others. Amuri was in her twenties. She was a student at Al-Najah University in the West Bank town of Nablus.

Terrorist wings

Political groups and terrorist groups are often linked. A 'terrorist wing' is a terrorist group that has links with a non-violent political group.

Hamas is the ruling party in Palestine. It has a terrorist wing, Hezbollah, that plots bombings.

Sinn Fein is a political party in Northern Ireland. It opposed British rule in Northern Ireland for many years. The IRA is Sinn Fein's terrorist wing. It killed around 1,800 people, between the late 1960s and early 1990s.

22

WOMEN AND TERRORISM

Women have always taken part in terrorism. But in the past they rarely carried out acts of violence. Today, however, the innocent appearance of women is being used as a tactic by more terrorist groups. Now, women suicide bombers are not uncommon.

A good disguise

Women are now common in terrorist groups such as the Basque Fatherland and Liberty (ETA) in Spain and the Revolutionary Armed Forces of Colombia (FARC) – see page 46. Women are helping terrorist groups to disguise themselves better. Women on their own (or a couple) are less likely to raise suspicion than two men working together.

Keeping the peace

Women have also tried to resolve the problems of terrorism. In the US, women are being used to question al-Qaeda suspects. In Northern Ireland, women have also been used to help with the ongoing peace process.

Leila Khaled

Leila Khaled was a Palestinian who attempted to hijack an Israeli flight in 1970. Khaled was arrested in the UK. She was released in exchange for western hostages held by the PFLP (see page 46). Khaled was four years old when her family were forced to leave Palestine when it was split in 1948. From a young age she committed herself to fight for the Palestinian cause.

Women in Black

Women in Black groups around the world are against war and other violence. These women often wear black. They try to educate people against acts of war.

In 1988, Women in Black groups were against Israel's occupation of the West Bank and the Gaza Strip. They demanded peace between Israelis and Palestinians. The idea has now spread around the world.

Women in Black groups carry out silent, non-violent protests in public places.

Women in Israel (above) and Iraq (top right) protest against terrorism. They hope for a peaceful world for all (right).

WORLD MAP OF TERRORISM

Nowhere is completely free from terrorism. In countries such as the US and parts of Europe, people live freely. This makes them vulnerable. Transport routes and supplies of water, electricity or fuel are also easy targets.

The developing world

The world's less developed nations are also experiencing a growing number of terrorist attacks. Many developing countries have weak central governments. They also go through times of civil war. These are ideal conditions for terrorist groups to seek power through force and the use of terror.

A growing problem

Domestic terrorism is a continuing problem in many unstable countries of the world. But today, an increase in international terrorism is becoming a major concern for world leaders. Terrorist groups around the world, such as al-Qaeda, have grown to support each other. Many groups are also finding a common cause in which they can work together.

The fight against the Taliban in 2001 saw the US and the UK work with the Northern Alliance in Afghanistan. They were looking for al-Qaeda suspects.

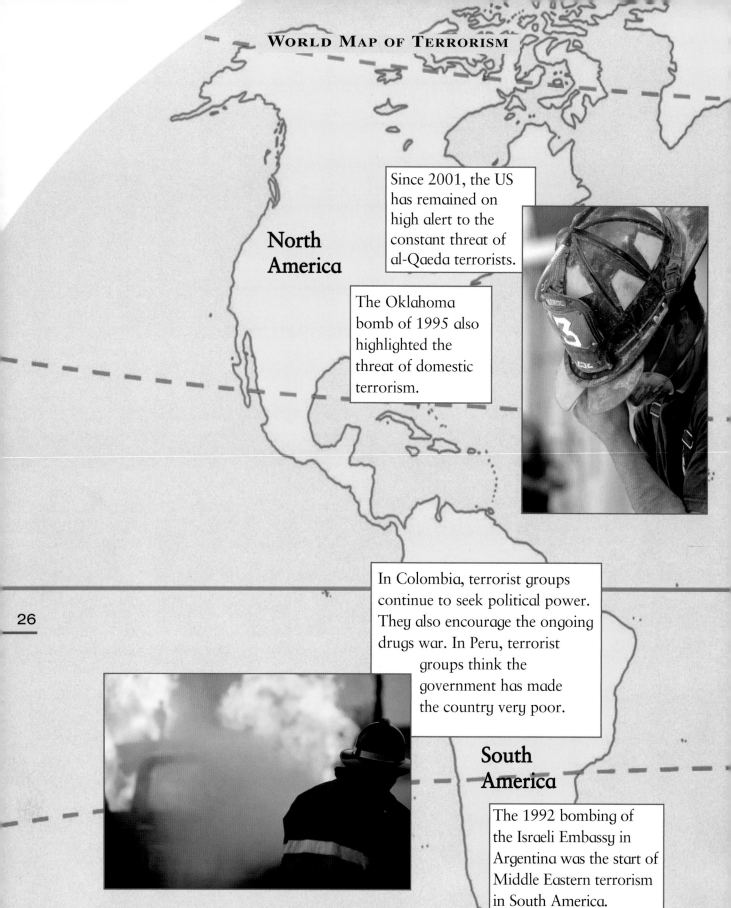

North
America

Since 2001, the US
has remained on
high alert to the
constant threat of
al-Qaeda terrorists.

The Oklahoma
bomb of 1995 also
highlighted the
threat of domestic
terrorism.

26

In Colombia, terrorist groups
continue to seek political power.
They also encourage the ongoing
drugs war. In Peru, terrorist
groups think the
government has made
the country very poor.

South
America

The 1992 bombing of
the Israeli Embassy in
Argentina was the start of
Middle Eastern terrorism
in South America.

Russia

In July 2005, London commuters became the target for suicide bombers, linked to al-Qaeda.

Europe

Chechen rebels have carried out a series of attacks against Russia.

The ETA have carried out a series of bloody attacks in Spain and France since the 1950s.

In 1995, a gas attack on the subway in Tokyo, Japan, killed 12 and injured more than 5,000.

Al-Qaeda groups are active in the Middle East. Terrorism in Israel continues, despite attempts at a peace process.

In 2006, trains in Mumbai, India, were bombed, killing 182 people.

Asia

Africa

Al-Qaeda-linked terrorists killed more than 88 people at a holiday resort in Egypt in 2005.

In Sri Lanka, the Tamil Tigers have carried out more than 200 suicide bombings since the late 1980s.

27

Jemaah Islamiah was blamed for the 2002 Bali bombing. The group has links with al-Qaeda.

Australia

World terrorism

From east to west, and north to south, terrorism is a very real threat to countries of the modern world.

THE FIGHT AGAINST TERRORISTS

There is no sure way to stop terrorism. Until a long-term solution is found, we must use short-term measures. These include tightening security.

Information helps governments to work out the risks of terrorism around the world.

Anti-terrorist police

The recent increase in terrorism has meant that additional resources have been given to police. They prepare for terrorist attacks and try to stop acts of terrorism.

Secret information

The use of secret information is very important in the fight against terrorism. This information is gathered from the media and from special agents such as spies. Governments get information from satellites and photography. They also monitor telephone or email conversations. Terrorists need money to carry out their activities. So stopping the bank accounts of suspect terrorist supporters can be very effective.

Reducing the risk

Anti-terrorist police and other government groups also set up emergency measures to reduce the impact of a terrorist attack. Emergency teams carry out regular drills to practise strategies in case a major evacuation is needed. They also tighten border controls and increase security on public transport and in other public places.

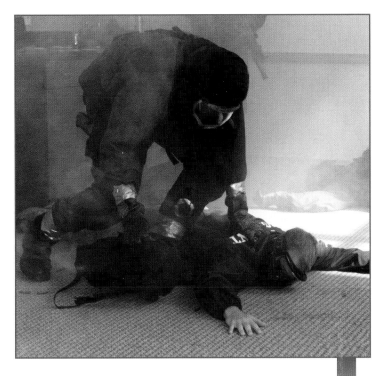

Anti-terrorist police carry out regular training.

Reacting to a threat

After September 11th, many countries developed strict security measures against the terrorist threat. After the 2005 attacks on the London public transport system, security measures were reviewed again. In August 2006, the threat of multiple bombings on flights to the US led to a full review of hand luggage policies on all airlines.

Preventing attacks

The work of anti-terrorist police has prevented a number of terrorist attacks. In January 2003, six men were arrested at a flat in London. Anti-terrorist police found small quantities of poison at the flat and the men were held for questioning.

In June 2003, Kenyan police stopped an al-Qaeda plot to bomb the US Embassy in Nairobi. When officials found information about the plot, they cancelled flights. The US Embassy was closed for four days.

In Israel, sniffer dogs are trained to find explosives.

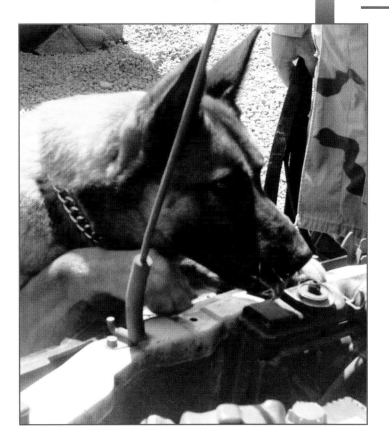

Long-term measures

Politicians are also looking at long-term measures to reduce the threat of terrorism. In countries such as Israel, where land is being disputed, nations have tried to introduce a peace process. They want to get the countries involved to talk. In some parts of the world, peace talks have helped to reduce levels of terrorism (see pages 34-38). This has encouraged other nations to try, too.

Stopping terrorism

Terrorism often occurs when people are unable to change attitudes in another, more peaceful way. If people continue to feel badly treated, new terrorist groups are likely to emerge.

In the long-term, terrorism will only be stopped when everyone can see another person's point of view. We all need to share the same values of human life regardless of political, religious or moral beliefs. An important part of that process is the development of a democratic system of government around the world. This system would allow all people to speak openly about their beliefs, without fear.

Ways to help

• Anti-terrorist police ask that people look out for suspicious items or activities.
• The public should let the police or other authorities know about anything suspicious.
• The police also ask that the public co-operate in the event of an attack. They should follow the instructions of those in charge of the emergency.

Terrorism and Human Rights

The rise in terrorism around the world has led to extreme measures to try to control the threat of terrorists. Human rights groups think that this is a threat to individual freedoms.

In many countries, people have to carry national identity cards.

The USA Patriot Act

In September 2001, the US government made a new law called the USA Patriot Act. Many people think this law is against freedom of speech. Its definition of 'domestic terrorism' could be seen to include non-violent protests. The Act also allows the government to look at emails and to get education and medical records, without permission.

Guantanamo Bay

Following the 2001 conflict in Afghanistan, the US have been holding over 600 people at a US naval base in Guantanamo Bay, Cuba. Human rights groups have called for the prisoners' release. In 2006, the US announced that it would close Guantanamo Bay.

Prisoners at Guantanamo Bay are Taliban fighters or al-Qaeda suspects. They are not allowed access to legal support.

Additional terrorist laws

Other countries have made laws to try to tighten security. In India, police can now hold suspects without charge. It is also illegal for journalists to meet with members of a terrorist group.

In China, the campaign against Islamic groups has been strengthened. These groups are thought to be linked to 'international terrorism'. In 2002, Australia increased the powers of the secret service. The government also made it illegal to become a member of a terrorist organisation.

In 2004, China began to issue identity cards for its population of over one billion people.

Tightening security measures

In Turkey, the government listens to some telephone conversations and raids private homes. This has angered human rights groups.

In many European countries, people have to carry national identity (ID) cards. Human rights groups are against these types of identification. They think that in a free society, people are allowed to have a certain level of privacy.

Other killers

There are many groups around the world that have frightened innocent people. The Italian Mafia is one of the world's oldest criminal organisations. Mafia groups have murdered

many people because of personal arguments. Most people think that Mafia groups are murderers, rather than terrorists. This is because they are not trying to change political policies by their actions.

A loss of freedom

The fear of terrorism has made new restrictions on freedom more acceptable. However, these restrictions are not new. In the 1970s and 80s, many human rights were overlooked in the UK. IRA suspects, for example, were often held for days without charge.

In March 1988, the British SAS shot dead three IRA members in Gibraltar. They thought the men were a threat. Britain later admitted the men were unarmed. In 1995, Britain was found to have broken the European Convention on Human Rights.

United Nations

• In 1945, the United Nations (UN) was formed to try to prevent another world war.
• In 1948, the UN passed the 'Universal Declaration of Human Rights' to help peace and justice.
• The UN has since developed rules to protect people's rights. The rules include measures against violence and torture. They also oppose discrimination against race, women or children.
• Each year the UN works with around 100 countries. It monitors the situation in these countries. It also recommends improvements in the area of human rights.

33

SOLUTIONS AND SUCCESSES

Peace talks have ended a number of terrorist campaigns. Politicians have to decide whether the reasons that people join terrorist organisations are understandable. This is the only way to begin rational peace talks.

Some governments have used peace talks to stop terrorism.

NORTHERN IRELAND

In the early 1990s, peace talks tried to resolve the conflict between Catholics and Protestants in Northern Ireland. In 1998, the talks resulted in the Good Friday Agreement. The British and Irish governments wanted peace. Most of the main political parties in Northern Ireland took part.

Finding a solution

The Good Friday Agreement suggested that minority Catholics in Northern Ireland should have a share of the political power. It also suggested that the Republic of Ireland in the south should be involved in Northern Irish affairs. In return, Catholics had to give up their idea of a united Ireland, unless the largely Protestant North voted in favour of it.

Sinn Fein leader, Gerry Adams (centre), took part in the Northern Ireland peace talks. He had previously been linked to terrorism.

The Irish Story

Ireland has had a difficult relationship with Britain for nearly 800 years. In the 12th century, Henry II of England invaded Ireland. Since then, there have always been groups wishing to make Ireland independent again. In 1916, Irish Nationalists declared an independent Irish Republic. This 'Easter Rising' was crushed by the British. The leaders were executed. This was the start of years of violence.

More than 3,600 Catholics and Protestants have died from acts of terrorism in Northern Ireland since 1969.

Living side by side

• There are two main groups in Northern Ireland. Unionists are mainly Protestants. They want Northern Ireland to stay part of the UK. Republicans are mainly Catholics. They want Northern Ireland to unite with the Republic of Ireland in the south. There are terrorist groups associated with both (see page 46).
• The IRA agreed to a cease-fire in 1994. In October 2001, the IRA began to disarm. Associated groups still remain, however.
• In 2006, broad agreement was reached to reopen the Northern Ireland Assembly.

A divided Ireland

After the Easter Rising, the Irish Republican Army (IRA) began a series of terrorist attacks. In 1920, the British and some Irish agreed to split Ireland into two. The south became an independent (mainly Catholic) area. The north (mainly Protestant) area remained part of the UK.

This split caused violence and terrorism for most of the 20th century. Catholics and Protestants could not find a way to resolve the situation.

35

Slow progress

In 2002, the Good Friday Agreement was under threat. There were reports that Sinn Fein members were still involved with the IRA. The IRA had also failed to disarm. The British government responded by suspending Northern Ireland's power-sharing government.

New negotiations began in 2004. Britain still thinks that Northern Ireland can become independent. There also seems to be no threat of further violence. As the talks continue, there is real hope that eventually there will be a lasting and fair solution to the troubles.

Good Friday Agreement

• On Good Friday 1998, an agreement was made to make peace in Northern Ireland.

• The result was the Belfast Agreement (commonly known as the Good Friday Agreement).

• The Good Friday Agreement meant the end of Britain's claim to Northern Ireland. It also set up a Northern Ireland Assembly that would share power.

• The Northern Ireland Assembly began in 1999. In 2002 it was suspended after problems with the peace process.

• Peace talks continue. In 2006, progress was made. The Northern Ireland Assembly is due to reopen at Stormont in 2007.

Pallbearers carry a victim of the Omagh bombing in Northern Ireland, 1998.

A changing South Africa

In 1912, community and church organisations in South Africa formed the African National Congress (ANC). The ANC wanted to protect the rights and freedoms of black South Africans. It started as a peaceful organisation. However, the South African government's policies against black communities became more serious. The ANC then turned to more violent methods.

SOUTH AFRICA

There have always been disagreements between black and white South Africans. However, tensions grew worse in the 20th century when white South African governments increased white control of the country. A policy called 'apartheid' made life difficult for black South Africans.

South Africa became a British colony in the 1800s. Then, during the 1900s, a policy of apartheid discriminated against black South Africans.

Peace turning to violence

Despite peaceful protests, the situation grew worse. In the 1940s, the African National Congress (ANC) started a more violent campaign. Many of the group were arrested. Peaceful protests continued in the 1950s. However, peace turned to anger in 1960, when police opened fire on a non-violent ANC related protest at Sharpville. Around 70 protesters were killed and almost 200 injured. In the following years the ANC carried out many violent acts. In 1964, the ANC leader Nelson Mandela was arrested. He was imprisoned for 27 years.

Mandela's release

Around the world, people wanted stronger actions against the South African government. They were also calling for Mandela's release.

In 1990, Nelson Mandela (left) was freed after 27 years in prison. In 1991, he was elected President of the ANC. Talks with the government resulted in the first elections for both black and white South Africans, in April 1994.

The ANC won these elections very easily. Then in May 1994, Nelson Mandela became the President of South Africa. He was now leader of the country he had spent his whole life trying to free.

'Free Mandela' campaign

In the 1980s, the ANC began the 'Free Mandela' campaign. Although the South African government resisted, the group protested in the streets. In 1990, the government was forced to lift their ANC ban.

38

Freedom fighters

The ANC wanted equal conditions for black South Africans. But they killed many people in the process. Some people think the ANC were terrorists. Others view their attacks as a part of the struggle against apartheid. Some people think it is even possible to be both terrorists and freedom fighters at the same time.

TERRORISM TODAY

News reports of the US terrorist attacks on September 11, 2001 and in London on July 7, 2005 made terrorism feel more real. Governments now want to show their nations that they are trying to keep people safe.

Today's weapons

Today, weapons are becoming more sophisticated. This is because materials are easier to obtain. One of the biggest threats is the 'dirty' bomb. This spreads radioactive material over a limited area. Other threats include the release of deadly chemicals or bacteria.

Subway attack

In 1995, members of Aum Shinrikyo, a Japanese religious cult, released sarin, a deadly nerve gas, into the Tokyo subway system. They killed 12 people and injured more than 5,000. This attack showed how easy it was for a small group to use chemical weapons.

Emergency teams wear protective clothing when they deal with the threat of chemical or biological attack.

Anthrax

Anthrax is a serious disease caused by bacteria. Anthrax is found naturally in the soil. However, today anthrax can also be made in a laboratory. Anthrax is treated with antibiotics.

Modern technology

Technology has helped governments to stop terrorists. However, it has also made it easier for terrorists to plan their activities. Modern technology is also a popular target for terrorists. Attacks on electronic equipment can cause a lot of damage.

Cyberterrorism

Cyberterrorism is a word used to describe a terrorist attack that interferes with computer networks. Small terrorist groups can use cheap computer equipment to disrupt larger computer networks. Cyberterrorists can have a wide impact without having to show their identity or their location. Targets include power stations, emergency services and banks.

40

Cyberterrorists are able to get past many security measures.

A second weapon

Cyberterrorism could be used by large terrorist organisations, such as al-Qaeda. Its use could make a conventional terrorist attack even worse. This would help to cause maximum devastation.

Sarin

Sarin is a very poisonous substance. It comes in both liquid and gas forms. Experts say that sarin gas can be produced by a trained chemist using chemicals that are available to the public.

Weapons of mass destruction

'Weapons of mass destruction' are weapons that cause widespread devastation. They include nuclear, chemical and biological weapons. A bomb containing nuclear material can make an area too dangerous to live in. Or it can actually destroy a whole city. Biological and chemical attacks release poison or bacteria.

A dirty bomb

The most common type of dirty bomb mixes an explosive with radioactive material. Such a bomb could fit into a suitcase (below). If the bomb explodes, many people would be hurt. Illnesses are also caused by exposure to radioactive material. Another type of dirty bomb could be hidden in a public place and release a powerful radioactive material.

Special showers are needed after a chemical or biological attack.

Al-Qaeda and Iraq

The greatest threat of weapons of mass destruction comes from the al-Qaeda network. Many believe that the events of September 11th show that modern terrorists are willing to kill on a large scale.

In 2003, the US and allied forces went to war with Iraq. They said that Saddam Hussein was helping al-Qaeda by producing 'weapons of mass destruction'. However, no evidence of this has been found.

TERRORISM IN THE FUTURE

We cannot be sure that terrorism will go away. There are always disagreements in the world. It takes years to work out some of the issues involved and to find a solution. But time is a healer. Many major disputes involving terrorist activities have been resolved in recent years.

Finding the answer

Terrorism has many causes. There will always be disputes about politics, land or beliefs. Terrorism is also influenced by events at the time. The ANC, for example, turned to violence in South Africa because black South Africans were being punished. This was at a time when other people in the world were free.

Looking for solutions

There is no single solution to terrorism. Conflicts can only be resolved when we find answers to the problems of a particular time and place. Negotiations in Northern Ireland and South Africa have made progress. However, a different combination needs to be found for Israelis and Palestinians, or for the threat of al-Qaeda.

In any part of the world, terrorism can cause serious damage and suffering.

Gathering information is important to prevent terrorist attacks.

Preventing terrorism

In the meantime, it is important that we prevent terrorists from carrying out their actions. Governments around the world must work together to always stay one step ahead of terrorists.

The September 11th attacks made us more aware and afraid of terrorism than ever before. However, most people will never come anywhere near an act of terrorism. The closest that most of us will ever get will still be the television pictures on the news. They make these violent acts feel like a real part of our lives.

43

Future generations may see an end to many of today's terrorism problems.

CHRONOLOGY

November 1605 – English Catholics tried to blow up the English Parliament in protest against their King, James I.

1795-1799 – The French Revolution saw the execution of many presumed enemies of the French government. This started the term 'terrorism'.

December 1920 – The British Parliament and some Irish agreed to split Ireland into one mainly Catholic area in the south and one mainly Protestant area in the north. The split caused violence for most of the 20th century.

May 1948 – The United Nations (UN) divided Palestine into two states – Palestine and Israel. The split has led to many acts of terrorism.

June 1964 – Nelson Mandela, leader of the African National Congress (ANC), was jailed for life for plotting to overthrow the South African government. Mandela was released 27 years later.

March 1979 – British politician Airey Neave was killed by a car bomb as he left the House of Commons. IRA-splinter groups were held responsible.

October 1984 – An IRA bomb caused devastation to the Grand Hotel in Brighton, UK, during the Conservative government's annual party conference. Four people died.

December 1988 – Libyan terrorists smuggled a bomb onto an aeroplane which exploded over Lockerbie, Scotland, UK. All 259 people on board were killed, as well as 11 people on the ground.

February 1993 – A car bomb exploded in an underground car park at the World Trade Center, New York City, killing six people.

March 1995 – A gas attack on the Tokyo subway killed 12 people and injured more than 5,000.

April 1995 – Timothy McVeigh bombed the Federal Building in Oklahoma City, USA, killing 168 and injuring more than 500.

July 1996 – A bomb exploded in Atlanta during the Olympic games, killing one and injuring over 100.

August 1998 – A car bomb exploded in Omagh, Northern Ireland, killing 29 people and injuring at least 220.

September 2001 – Two hijacked planes crashed into the World Trade Center, New York City. The Pentagon, in Washington, was struck by a third hijacked plane. A fourth plane crashed into a field in southern Pennsylvania. In total, over 3,000 lives were lost. Osama bin Laden is thought to be the prime suspect.

December 2001 – A US flight made an emergency landing. Richard Reid, a passenger, had tried to set light to explosives in his shoes. Reid was sentenced to life in prison in 2003.

October 2002 – Two car bombs exploded in Bali, killing over 200 people.

July 2005 – Suicide bombers trained by al-Qaeda blew up three underground trains and a bus in London, killing 53 people.

July 2006 & February 2007 – Train bomb attacks in India (in Mumbai in 2006 and near Panipat in 2007) killed over 200 people.

August 2006 – Plans were discovered to blow up at least 11 airliners flying from the UK to the US. Suspected al-Qaeda members were arrested.

March 2007 – Unionists and Sinn Fein agreed to share power in Northern Ireland.

ORGANISATIONS AND GLOSSARY

African National Congress (ANC)
The ANC was formed in 1912 to defend the rights of black South Africans.

Al-Qaeda
A terrorist organisation that wants to create an international Islamic state. The group is behind some of the major international terrorist attacks of the 21st century.

Basque Fatherland and Liberty (ETA)
ETA was formed in 1959. It wants independence for the Basque region of north-western Spain. Targets include police officers, soldiers, and the tourist industry.

Chechen rebels
Terrorists from Chechnya who want political independence from Russia.

Hamas (Islamic Resistance Movement)
An Islamic group that wants an independent Palestinian state.

Hezbollah (Party of God)
A radical Islamic group from Lebanon.

Irish Republican Army (IRA)
The largest of the terrorist groups that fought for a united Ireland in the 1900s.

Liberation Tigers of Tamil (LTTE)
The LTTE wants an independent state in areas of Sri Lanka where Tamils live. Also known as the Tamil Tigers.

Palestine Liberation Organisation (PLO)
The PLO, formed in 1964, fight for the territorial rights of Palestinians.

Popular Front for the Liberation of Palestine (PFLP)
The PFLP is opposed to talks with Israel over the occupation of Palestine.

Red Army Faction (Baader-Meinhof gang)
A communist terror group which used to act in Germany.

Revolutionary Armed Forces of Colombia (FARC)
FARC was set up in 1964 as the military wing of the Colombian Communist Party. FARC has attacked political, military and economic targets in their war against the state.

Ulster Volunteer Force (UVF)
The leading terrorist organisation in Northern Ireland. It wants to keep political unity with the UK.

Apartheid – A political system set up in South Africa. It stopped black people from having basic rights.

Assassination – The murder of an important person, such as a politician, by a surprise attack.

Cyberterrorism – Terrorism that attacks modern technology.

Democracy – A political system that allows choice and power to be shared amongst all people.

Dirty bomb – A bomb used to scatter biological or radioactive chemicals throughout an area.

Freedom fighter – The term used for a terrorist who uses violent methods to overturn an unfair government or political system.

Fundamentalist – Someone who uses religion in an extreme way.

Hijacking – When a terrorist takes charge of an aeroplane, train or boat. This is against the wishes of the pilot, driver or captain.

Hostages – People held against their will. Demands are often made in exchange for their release.

Islam – The religion founded by the prophet Mohammad in the 7th century. A person who follows Islam is called a Muslim.

Mafia – An international secret organisation set up in Sicily in the 19th century. The group is involved in many illegal operations. These include drug smuggling, gambling and corruption.

Mujahideen – The Islamic term for somebody who fights in a jihad (a holy war).

Osama bin Laden – The leader of the al-Qaeda network.

Shah – A Shah was once a ruler in some Middle Eastern countries.

Special Air Service (SAS) – Part of the British Army. The SAS is involved with secret activities, such as fighting terrorism.

Taliban – The strict fundamentalist Islamic group that took charge of Afghanistan in 1996.

United Nations (UN) – An international organisation founded in 1945 to promote peace, security and economic development.

47

INDEX

48

Picture Research: Brian Hunter Smart **Photo Credits:** Abbreviations: l-left, r-right, b-bottom, t-top, c-centre, m-middle
Front cover, 39tr — M P Shelato/USMC. 1 all, 4mr, 6tr, 7mr, 8bl, 11tr, 14ml, 15br, 16tl, 18 both, 19tl, 21tr, 22bl, 23tr, 26bl, 30tr, 33tr, 34tr, 36tr, 40tl, 40br, 41ml — Photodisc. 2bl, 13c, 14tr — FEMA. 2-3b, 43tl — Lisa Borges/US Navy. 3tr, 22tl — Cherie A Thurlby/US Airforce. 4tr — David Salazar/US Navy. 4bl, 36bl — Alan Lewis/CORBIS SYGMA. 5bl, 6c, 30br, 45tr — Andrea Booher/FEMA. 7tl — D Faram/US Navy. 7c — Ted Banks/US Navy. 9tl, 20tr, 27c, 32t, 37tr, 37c, 38tl, 38br — Corel. 9br — Andre Brutman/Israeli Government Press Office. 10br — Ohayon Avi/Israeli Government Press Office. 11bl — David Turnley/CORBIS. 12tr, 35c, 37tl — Corbis. 12b, 25mr — Johnny Bivera/US Navy.14br — Ralf-Finn Hestoft/CORBIS. 16bl — Aaron Peterson/US Navy. 17tl — Alek Malhas/US Navy. 17ml — Bryn Colton/Assignments Photographers/CORBIS. 19br — Steve W Kirtley/USMC. 20ml, 41bl — Flat Earth. 21ml — US Navy. 23br — Bettman/CORBIS. 24ml — Gregory K Funk/USMC. 24mr — Arlo K Abrahamson/US Navy. 24bm — Anthony R Blanco/USMC. 26tr, 29tl — Jim Watson/US Navy. 28mr, 45bl — Adam Johnston/US Airforce. 29br — Matthew A Apprendi/USMC. 31tr — PBD. 31br — Shane T McCoy/US Navy. 34bl, 35tr — Peter Turnley/CORBIS. 39bl, 41tr — Bill Lisbon/USMC. 40tr — Joseph R Chenelly/USMC. 42b — Eric J Tilford. 43r — Matthew Orr/US Navy. 44tr — Nathan Alan Heusdens/USMC. 44bl — Digital Stock.